EXPLORING GOD'S MERCY

Five images of salvation

STEVEN CROFT

CHURCH HOUSE
PUBLISHING

Church House Publishing
Church House
Great Smith Street
London SW1P 3AZ

ISBN 978 0 7151 4224 0

Published 2010 by Church House Publishing

British Library Cataloguing in Publication data

A catalogue record for this book is available from the British Library

978 0 7151 4224 0

Cover design by Leigh Hurlock
Inside design by Hugh Hillyard-Parker, Edinburgh
Printed in England by Halstan

CONTENTS

INTRODUCTION

This book aims to help you understand how much God loves you.

One of life's biggest challenges is to grasp this one simple truth: God loves *you*. God loves you passionately, deeply and unconditionally. God's love for you does not depend on anything you do or anything you become. You cannot earn God's love. God knows you and God loves you.

Love is a rich concept. There are many different words for love in the Bible. One of the main ones can be translated as 'steadfast love' or 'mercy' or 'covenant love'. It is love that is stronger than death and does not waver whatever the circumstances.

It sounds as though it should be a very easy thing to understand God's steadfast love and mercy. But in fact God's mercy is very profound. It takes a lifetime to get to know it well.

Last year I moved to Sheffield, and my house is on the edge of the Peak District. I've never lived near this part of England before and hardly know it at all. I thought at first the Peak District was quite a small place: something I could explore in a day or two. In fact, it's a vast area of natural beauty. It divides into around five different areas: the Southern Dales, the Western Moors, the White Peak, the Derwent Valley and the Dark Peak. Each is very different. Each will take many weeks to explore properly. I'm looking forward to that.

In the same way, it takes many years to explore God's mercy: the depth and the ways and the constancy and the strength of God's love for you. This book and the short series of studies aim to take you further on that journey. The book can be read by yourself with the exercises used for personal reflection. However, it's best read as part of a small group. Each chapter is structured as material for a small group of people to work through in Lent or any other season of the year. Each chapter (and each group study) has three main elements:

- a reading from Psalm 107
- a testimony based on Mark 4—9
- a New Testament passage on the passion of Christ.

Psalm 107: Exploring God's mercy through five images

Each chapter begins with a reading and reflection on part of Psalm 107. Psalm 107 is one of the longer psalms of praise. From beginning to end, the psalm explores God's mercy through a series of very vivid images and pictures. The psalm opens with a call to give thanks to the LORD for his steadfast love (or mercy), which endures for ever (Psalm 107.1). The psalm ends with the invitation to consider or to explore the mercy of the LORD (Psalm 107.41).

The main part of the psalm is unique. It is structured around five very striking songs of testimony to God's love. Different groups of people are summoned from every part of the world to sing about this everlasting, active and wonderful mercy. The psalm helps us explore God's mercy by looking at these five different experiences of grace and love and salvation. As I picture the psalm being used in the temple, I like to think of five different choirs stepping forward for each song.

- The first part of the psalm is the **Song of the Pilgrim Way** (vv. 4–9). This song explores the mercy of God through the experience of being lost and then found; hungry and then satisfied.

- The second song is the **Song of Freedom** (vv. 10–16), which explores the mercy of God through the experiences of being held prisoner and then set free.

- The third song is the **Song of Wholeness** (vv. 17–22), which explores the mercy of God through the experiences and imagery of being sick and being made well again.

- The fourth song is the **Song of Calm** (vv. 23–32), which explores the mercy of God through the experience of being caught in a storm at sea and finding your way home again to safe harbour.

- The fifth song (vv. 33–38) is slightly different. It is not so much a testimony in which people look back and give thanks, as a statement on God's mercy and power. I have called this song the **Song of Fruitfulness**, and it explores the mercy of God through the contrast between the barren and the fruitful life.

Each of the five great pictures in these five songs gives us a window in God's steadfast love. They are images of our salvation. They are five pathways to follow to explore what God's love for us means: a walk through a different part of the Peak District, if you like.

As Christians of every generation, we have been lost and now we are found and on the Way. We have been held captive and now we are set free. We have been sick in mind and spirit and are made whole again. We have been storm tossed and engulfed by chaos but we have come to the place of peace. We have been barren but now we bear fruit in our lives. These are images of salvation because of what we have been saved from (confusion, captivity, death, chaos and frustration) and what we are saved for (the journey with God, freedom, life, peace and fulfilment).

The psalm was not written for one specific group of lost people or prisoners. The Psalms in general put into words for us the deepest experiences of our lives: whether of joy or sorrow. This psalm gives God's people words to explore the wonderful truth of God's great love through the five profound pictures of grace.

Psalm 107 explores God's mercy. Because of God's mercy, the lost are found and the hungry are fed. Because of God's mercy, the prisoners are set free. Because of God's mercy, the diseased are made well. Because of God's mercy, the overwhelmed find safe harbour. Because of God's mercy, the barren become fruitful.

We can take this further and make it much more personal. Because of God's mercy, when I was lost and hungry, God found me and nourished me. When I was trapped and in chains, God's love set me free. When I was sick in spirit and diseased, God healed me. When I am overwhelmed, God leads me to safe harbour. When my life is barren, God leads me on again to a place of fruitfulness.

The pictures in the songs tell us something about what it is like to live without knowing God's love. We all know something of what it is like to be lost and hungry, trapped, diseased in our spirits, overwhelmed and barren. These pictures enable us to think more deeply about the difference God's love and mercy makes to us.

In each part of our journey, Psalm 107 is the starting point, the window we look through to see one view, one perspective on God's mercy.

Mark 4—9: Exploring God's mercy through the ministry of Jesus

We then move on to look at the way in which each image of God's mercy is revealed in a deeper way in the life and ministry of Jesus. As Christians we believe that Jesus is God in human form, who shows to us all what God is like. In Jesus, God's mercy and steadfast love is revealed in its clearest form.

There are many passages from the gospels we could choose for each of the five pictures of grace. I have chosen five passages from the early chapters of St Mark's gospel. Some scholars believe that there is a close relationship between Psalm 107 and these chapters of Mark: each image from the psalm seems to be woven carefully and deliberately into this section of the gospel. The more I have reflected on Psalm 107, the more I have agreed with them. I've explored these passages in this book through an imaginative testimony and re-telling of the events which forms part of each chapter.

The passion story: exploring God's mercy through the death and resurrection of Jesus

Finally we will move on to look through each of these windows of mercy and images of grace at a different aspect of the great story of Jesus' death and resurrection.

We believe that we know and receive God's love through the death of Jesus on the cross and his resurrection from the dead. The great Prayer of Thanksgiving in the Church of England's prayer book speaks very eloquently of 'all the benefits of his passion'. We will explore together just some of the benefits and blessings that come to us and to all who will receive them because of Jesus' death on the cross.

The death and resurrection of Jesus provide the way for the lost to be found, the hungry fed, the prisoners set free, the diseased healed, and the barren fruitful. To explore the meaning of the cross is to explore God's mercy.

For this part of each chapter I have chosen passages from the whole of the New Testament, not simply from the Gospel accounts of the passion. As the early Christians reflected on the meaning of the events of Good Friday and Easter Day, they were inspired by the Spirit and by the Old Testament Scriptures to see the promises of salvation made possible in Christ's death and resurrection.

This in turn makes it possible for us to see more clearly through the windows of grace how great and mighty is God's love for us and how much our life can be transformed through the death and resurrection of Jesus Christ.

Prayer and reflection

Exploring God's mercy is not like learning about Henry VIII, or the properties of plutonium. It's not, in other words, just about learning some new facts or texts or connections.

Exploring God's mercy is about getting to know God more fully and therefore understanding the power and the wonder of his love and his love for each of us. That in turn will lead to change.

For this reason, each session is set in the context of prayer. I've provided a suggested order of prayer for the beginning of each session on page 9. At the end of the session I have suggested an order of prayer.

You will also find scattered through the book some ideas for personal reflection, which you can use as part of your own prayers through the five studies. Many Christians find it worthwhile to keep a journal: to write down in an exercise book or on the computer particular prayers or insights that are helpful. This grows over time into a valuable tool to guide you in your walk with God.

Why explore God's mercy?

Each week, the study begins with this beautiful prayer from the letter to the Ephesians. You may know it very well but take a moment to read it slowly and carefully now.

> I pray that you may have the power to comprehend, with all the saints, what is the breadth and length and height and depth, and to know the love of Christ that surpasses knowledge, so that you may be filled with all the fullness of God.
>
> *Ephesians 3.18–19*

Paul clearly believes that it is not an easy thing to understand how much God loves us. It does not come naturally. It is not a solitary exercise. We need to 'comprehend with all the saints'. It is not simply a matter of applying our minds to the task. We need spiritual insight. We need God to reveal himself to us – to show us his love. Nor is it an exercise that leaves us unchanged. As we explore God's mercy we ourselves are changed – filled with all the fullness of God.

Why does Paul pray this prayer for the Ephesians and for Christians in every age? Because to know the extent of God's love for us and for all the world is the best news in the world. The Christian life is often difficult. It involves sacrifice. Life itself involves suffering. We are strengthened to live the Christian life well as we explore God's love and mercy. We catch a glimpse of God's higher purpose, of his vision for creation, of the wonder in each day.

Exploring God's mercy leads us to a greater love of God himself and also greater love for our neighbours. The more we know and understand of God's love, the more we will speak of it to others. The more we know and understand of God's love, the more we will be willing to see other people as dearly loved by God also and be willing to serve them. The more we know and understand what God has done for us, the more we will offer our own lives back to God.

Roots

The theme for this book emerged from reading and reflecting on Psalm 107 over a number of years. However, it also has its roots in a particular experience of God's grace and love.

Five years ago, I was given the gift of a sabbatical after more than 20 years of ministry. I was passing through something of a dry time in my spiritual journey. One of my hopes for the sabbatical was that I would learn to listen to God again and that our friendship would grow. I set aside time each day for that listening and friendship.

What did I hear? Well, there was silence. I heard nothing at all for about eight or nine weeks. It wasn't an uncomfortable silence. I had an inner peace and a sense I was doing what I ought to be doing: waiting and attending to see what God might say to me. But it was silence. At the beginning of the time I had a number of important questions in my mind. There were key life decisions to be taken. As the weeks went by, I learned to put them to the back of my mind and simply to wait.

Finally, towards the end of the sabbatical, the silence was broken. Out of the silence God spoke again. He said one word to me. The word was powerful and life-shaping and deep and clear. That one word was all I needed to hear. Five years later, that one word continues to give me life.

'Beloved.'

Brothers and sisters, let's explore together the mercy of the LORD.

INTRODUCTORY NOTES FOR GROUP LEADERS

You will need a copy of this book for each member of the group. Ideally they should have the chance to read it a few weeks before you begin to study it together.

There are notes for group leaders at the beginning of each session to guide you through. It's pretty self explanatory.

> The book is designed to be used with five short films for small groups and individuals, which introduce the theme of each chapter. You will find links to these films – which are freely available on YouTube – along with sound files of this material at **www.chpublishing.co.uk/exploringgodsmercy**

Feel free to mix and match the different elements in the session to suit your own group. The material should work well with an existing home group or one that comes together just for Lent or at some other time of the year.

You will need to be selective. Try to focus the time on the interactive parts of the session.

There are practical activities each week that require a bit of preparation and some simple equipment. These are detailed in the leader's notes.

Each session should begin with the opening prayers on page 9 to begin the study, and then move straight into the reading of the psalm.

Different ways to use the material

Over ten weeks not five

Not every group has 90 minutes they can use for this kind of study. You could divide each session into two parts. Focus on the material and exercises from Psalm 107 in the first part and then next week look at the material from Mark's gospel.

In twos and threes

Not everyone is able to be part of a small group. You could work through the material in Lent with two or three friends, or as a married couple, or as an older Christian working with someone who is new to the faith. You will need to read the chapters carefully and think about them.

As a congregation

Not every church has a tradition of midweek home meetings. You could also use the materials as part of a midweek Eucharist in Lent:

● The opening prayers could be used as the Preparation for the service.

● The two readings would be the psalm section and the gospel text (not the retelling here).

● After a short reflection (which could be the YouTube clip) the congregation could divide into groups to discuss the material and pray for one another.

● The congregations would draw together again for the Peace and for Communion.

● Parts of the closing prayers could be used at the end.

Clearly you could not use all the material in the chapters as part of a Eucharist. Focus on the images in Psalm 107 and leave people to read through the sections on Mark's gospel and the reflections on the passion on their own.

On your own

Finally, the book is also intended to be read by individuals. If you are working through it on your own, make sure you use the times and spaces for prayer and for journaling.

God will be at work!

However you engage with the material, remember that God in his grace will be at work in you and in the other people who explore these passages. It is very powerful and life changing indeed to explore the extent of God's love for us.

OPENING PRAYERS TO BEGIN THE SESSION

If you are using this book as a group, these opening prayers should be used at the very beginning of each meeting. If you are working through this book on your own, the prayers should be used at the start of each chapter.

A candle is lit as a sign of God's presence and light. We say together the words in bold type.

> Give thanks to the LORD for he is good
> **For his mercy lasts for ever**
>
> Let the redeemed of the LORD give testimony
> **Those he has saved from the hand of their enemy**
>
> The LORD has gathered us from all the earth
> **From east and west, from the north and from the chaos of the seas**
>
> *Psalm 107.1–3*

The group keep a time of silent thanksgiving for the signs of God's mercy in our lives. After one minute of silence, one or more people should lead in a time of thanksgiving.

A hymn or song can be played or sung together.

This prayer is said together:

> **Almighty Father, out of your glorious riches**
> **Strengthen our hearts by your Holy Spirit**
> **Grant us power with all the saints**
> **To appreciate how wide and long and high and deep**
> **Is the love of Christ**
> **Help us to know this love which surpasses knowledge**
> **And fill us to overflowing with all the fullness of God.**
> **Amen**
>
> *From Ephesians 3.16–19*

After these opening prayers, move straight to the reading at the start of this week's chapter.

NOTES ON THE OPENING REFRAIN

We will use the first three verses of Psalm 107 at the start of each session. **Verse 1** calls us to give thanks. God has done so much for us and our response should be one of appreciation and wonder. But praise does not come as naturally to us as grumbling and complaining. That's why we need to practise. Life often teaches us to criticize others. We need the disciplines of worship and thanksgiving to learn to enjoy all that God has given us.

This first verse is also like a creed. We come together, perhaps after a hard day or a difficult week. We remember that despite all that we may have seen, God is good and his mercy lasts for ever. At some times when life is going very well, these words will be very easy and natural to say. At other times of pain and difficulty they will be much more difficult. One of the great strengths of Christian community is that at any one time some of us will be in a good place and others in a harder one: we help and support one another.

God is addressed throughout this Psalm by his personal name. This name is revealed to Moses in Exodus 3.14. This name is so holy that it is never pronounced by the Jews. In English Bibles the convention is to write the LORD in capitals instead of this name. However, we should remember as we read the words that we are called to a personal relationship with the LORD, to be on first-name terms, as it were, and to know him well.

The word translated 'mercy' here is a special one in the Bible. It means God's strong and steadfast love, his commitment to us, his strong regard, his grace. This love is stronger than we can ever appreciate. It is love we have done nothing to earn and do not deserve. It is deeper than the oceans, higher than the mountains, wider than the east is from the west. The whole task of our Christian lives is about appreciating how much God loves us.

Verse 2 calls on the redeemed of the LORD to speak out, to give testimony. What does it mean to be the redeemed of the LORD? The word redeemed means bought back or rescued. Today we might get some sense of what the word means by trying to imagine a person being bought from a slave market or a valuable object redeemed from the pawnbroker's shop and beautifully restored.

As Christians we believe we are redeemed by God through the death of Jesus on the cross. In Ephesians we read:

> In him we have redemption through his blood, the forgiveness of
> our trespasses, according to the riches of his grace ...
>
> *Ephesians 1.7*

As we will explore together, we have been saved from many enemies. God has rescued us and is putting us back together. As we will see from the psalm these enemies are not personal but universal. Part of the human condition is to do battle with the things that enslave us or overwhelm us or seek to destroy us. They are enemies like slavery to sin and death and chaos and a wasted, barren life.

These enemies together draw us towards the scrap heap, the rubbish dump, the place where everything is abandoned and they leave us there. One of the strongest images for hell in the Bible is the Valley of Ben Hinnom, the vast rubbish dump outside the city of Jerusalem: the scrap heap. Without God's love and mercy we are on the scrap heap – drawn there by destructive forces at work within us and within creation. But God has not abandoned us to that fate. He sends his Son, Jesus Christ, to salvage us. He buys us back from the scrap yard and lovingly restores us in his image. Jesus' death on the cross is the price of our redemption and the way in which we are restored.

So now we can sing this song together as people who are redeemed by Christ. As the Church, we are the people gathered by Christ from every corner of the earth, an international community. One day we will sing these great songs of salvation together in heaven. Now we sing together in smaller gatherings as we travel together on this earth.

Most English translations keep the four points of the compass in **verse 3**. However, the Hebrew says clearly: from east and west, from the north and from the sea. The sea may be simply another word for 'south'. However, later in the psalm, the sea is a symbol of chaos and disorder in our lives, of forces that overwhelm us (vv. 23–32). Usually the sea stands for this kind of chaos in the Old Testament (think of the waters moving over the earth in Genesis 1.1). For that reason I have kept the original term in the translation we will use.

The sessions are about learning to appreciate God's love in new ways. For that reason the opening prayers contain three exercises. Think of them as a kind of warm-up stretch before you do a session at the gym. The first is a time for silent prayer together, each person saying thank you to the LORD in their own heart and in their own way. The second is a chance for one or more people to pray out loud, thanking God for specific blessings. The third is the opportunity to listen to music or to sing together.

The final part of the opening prayers is a short prayer to say together, which is based on one of Paul's prayers in Ephesians 3. It's a prayer that God will help us as we explore his mercy and understand more of the love of Christ.

LOST AND FOUND; HUNGRY AND SATISFIED

notes for leaders

You will need to give some time at the beginning to explain the purpose of the studies and, if this is a new group, to enable people to introduce themselves (or talk in pairs and introduce one another).

Approximate timings for the session are:

Welcome; opening prayers and reflection	15 mins
Sharing your story	15 mins
Film or song clip	5 mins
A testimony (reading and reflection)	10 mins
Sharing together	20 mins
A reflection on the passion and discussion	15 mins
Final worship and prayers together	10 mins

There is a lot of material in each session so you will need to select from week to week.

Not every group will have 90 minutes available. You could take a couple of evenings over each session. The first would look at the psalm material; the second at the gospel story and the reflection on the passion.

Additional activities

There is a short film clip available on YouTube, and a sound file on the Church House Publishing website, which introduce the session. If you decide to use them, they can be played after the initial reading of Psalm 107. To find the clip on YouTube go to **www.chpublishing.co.uk/exploringgodsmercy** and follow the link. Please visit the same page to find a downloadable sound file you may wish to use instead.

The session suggests sharing warm bread together. It may be that a member of the group can bake a loaf for the session or that you could have an automatic breadmaker timed to have the bread ready for exactly the right moment.

Involving the group

You may want to involve different members of the group in:

● Leading the opening and closing worship.

● Providing the bread and other refreshments.

● Reading the story (perhaps with several voices).

Other media

A good image of wandering through the wilderness would be from Sam and Frodo's wanderings through Mordor from *The Lord of the Rings: The Return of the King.*

For a song track that evokes the restlessness of modern life play Lily Allen, 'The Fear' (but note that the song contains some powerful language even in the single version).

You may be able to think of other clips that illustrate being hungry or lost.

If you need to explore a little more the idea of this book and the great images of salvation, then use the hymn 'Amazing Grace' or the Neil Diamond track, 'Pretty Amazing Grace', which both use some of the images from the psalm.

LOST AND FOUND; HUNGRY AND SATISFIED

Begin with the opening prayers on page 9.

The Song of the Pilgrim Way

Some wandered in wilderness and desert
They lost their way home to a place where they could live

They were hungry and thirsty
and their life force ebbed away

Then they cried out to the LORD in their distress
He saved them from all their troubles

He led them by a straight pathway
To a place where they could make their home

Let them give thanks to the LORD for he is good
For the wonders he does for the human race

For he satisfies the thirsty soul
And the hungry heart he fills with good things.

Psalm 107.4–9

Part 1 Exploring God's mercy through the Song of the Pilgrim Way

Most of us know what it's like to be lost or take a wrong turning. Most of us can remember a time when we had to miss a meal or two and felt hungry. Both of these feelings are symbols of what life is like without God's love and mercy.

For many people, life really is like being lost in a parched desert, stranded and unable to find the way home. There is a lack of direction in life and there is no way to navigate. Hunger and thirst set in: a longing for something more, something new, something that satisfies.

There is a sense in the dryness of daily life of restlessness and discontent. We long for something better. We have a sense of being not truly at home here.

Different people address that inner lostness in different ways. Some try and satisfy the spiritual hunger and thirst by trying to become rich only to find that physical food and drink do not satisfy. Some deal with their restlessness by constantly wandering from one place or relationship to another. Some imagine that if only they reach their next goal then everything will fall into place.

Others try to deaden the longing with drink or drugs or sex. Most people just give up and lose hope that things could ever be different. We learn to live with our lostness and our discontent. Spiritual hunger becomes a way of life.

Still others have no way to navigate through life: no strong principles or values; no moral compass; no way of choosing or making decisions. As their life goes on and difficulties come upon them they simply come to feel more and more lost. Sooner or later, the scrap heap gets them.

The people of Israel had a strong sense of what it meant to be lost and wander in the desert handed down to them. Each generation learned the stories of the Exodus in which a whole people wandered in the wilderness yet was guided and sustained by God's presence. They also had a strong sense of what it meant to depend on God for food and drink in the wilderness. Exodus tells of the gift of manna, which fed the people each day on their journey. It tells of the miraculous gifts of water and quails (see Exodus 16 and 17 for some of these stories).

The psalmists use this language of being hungry and thirsty for God in powerful ways:

> As a deer longs for flowing streams, so my soul longs for you,
> O God.
> My soul thirsts for God, for the living God.
>
> *Psalm 42.1*

> O God, you are my God, I seek you,
> my soul thirsts for you; my flesh faints for you,
> as in a dry and weary land where there is no water.
>
> *Psalm 63.1*

As well as this strong sense of longing, there are also psalms that reflect an equally strong sense of being at home; of being satisfied; of complete trust in God.

> For God alone my soul waits in silence;
> from him comes my salvation.
>
> *Psalm 62.1*

> But I have calmed and quieted my soul, like a weaned child
> with its mother;
> my soul is like the weaned child that is with me.
>
> *Psalm 131.2*

The Song of the Pilgrim Way contains a very deep truth in the third verse (Psalm 107.6) in the little word 'then'. The early stages of feeling lost in the desert don't feel too bad. You think, perhaps, that you will find the way back to civilization sooner or later. You will find before too long some food or drink that satisfies.

But then disaster strikes. The life force begins to ebb away. You realize that there is no way to get home with your own resources. It is at that moment that people cry to the LORD in their trouble and seek help.

You may know the story Jesus tells of the two sons in Luke 15. At what point does the younger son turn around and head for home? He has been lost and hungry for some time. His money has run out. There is a famine in the land. He tries at first to sort his own life out by taking work feeding the pigs.

It's only when he reaches the end of his own inner resources that he turns round on the inside and decides to head for home. When he does, he finds his father looking out for him and waiting to welcome him in. He is the one who satisfies the thirsty soul and fills the hungry heart with good things.

The verse at the end of the Song of the Pilgrim Way is quoted directly in the New Testament in the song of Mary, often called the Magnificat: he has filled the hungry with good things.

Sharing your story

Take some moments to reflect on how your life was (or is) without God. You may be able to look back to a time when you were not a Christian. You may not be sure that you are a Christian now. You may always have had a faith but you may have had times when you wandered away from God.

Tell part of your story to one another using the language of being lost and spiritually hungry and thirsty. What was it like? How did you find your way home?

Do you experience in your Christian life now times of dryness and hunger and times when you don't know God's direction?

You may want to share as a whole group; or one person might prepare in advance and tell part of their story; or you might want to share in twos or threes.

If you are reading this book on your own take some time at this point to journal and look back on the way this sense of being lost or being hungry and thirsty has surfaced in your life.

A film or song clip

See page 16 for suggestions.

Part 2 Exploring God's mercy in the ministry of Jesus

A testimony

One of the group should read the story aloud.

> I was 19 at the time. I remember it just like yesterday. Summertime. A bit of a holiday. Normal kind of thing. Larking around in the wine

bars by the shore. There were six of us. None of us could settle. We were restless all that summer.

Some wanted to leave town and go to the big city. Most of us stayed put: wanting the adventure but too frightened to go. Some had married already. I was still single at the time. I'd tried a few jobs. Nothing seemed to last. I thought about the army. My mum was worried sick but I never saw it at the time.

We saw a boat crossing the lake from where we sat by the shore. It was coming in on the far side in the middle of nowhere. The rumour went round it was this man Jesus. He was just starting to pull in the crowds.

'Wanna go?' said one of the lads. 'Can't be bothered,' I said. But the rest were up for it, so we joined the crowds streaming out of the city. Late morning it was. We'd not eaten.

It's further round that lake than you might think. By the time we got to where the boat had come ashore it was late afternoon. We had another hour to walk into the hills. The whole of our town was there plus a couple more. It was baking hot. Every so often we'd see someone exhausted by the side of the road or heading back down to the lake.

I was parched by this time and really hungry. No one had any food. There was nowhere to buy anything. We were miles from anywhere.

We couldn't hear much at the back of the crowd so we crept nearer round the edge. He was telling stories. They were good ones. Made me think. A couple of hours went by and we hardly noticed.

But then night began to come in. You could tell some of the people were worried. They'd been out all day in the sun. No one had been expecting this.

A couple of his friends thought so too. They tried to persuade him to stop and send the people away. Everyone was hungry. You could sense the holiday atmosphere beginning to change. There was an ugliness just below the surface.

I was close enough to hear by now. He told them to go and sort out something to eat for the crowd, testing them. They said it was impossible. They had neither bread nor money for this crowd.

'So how much do you have?' he asked.

'Five loaves,' they said. 'And two fish.'

He looked at them and smiled. 'Get everyone to sit down,' he said, as if there was going to be a party. People were starting to leave you see. Sundown wasn't far away.

So they did – we all had to sit in groups of about fifty or a hundred right across the valley.

Jesus stood right in the middle where everyone could see him. He took this small basket of food and he lifted it up to heaven and gave thanks to God. Then he lowered the basket and started breaking the loaves and putting the broken bread into twelve other baskets, which had appeared from nowhere.

The crowd was really quiet. Each of the disciples took one of the baskets out to a section of the crowd and began to pass out the bread and the fish. When the basket was empty he went back to Jesus. Jesus was still breaking up the bread and fish in the original basket. On and on it went. The food was passed from hand to hand. It was good strong bread as fresh as if it had just come from the bakery. The fish was good too. Everyone ate as much as they could. The water bottles were passed round. We were stuffed.

After the feast the disciples moved around talking to people. No one could explain it. They dismissed the crowd, who were amazed. Everyone moved off. I stayed behind and watched what would happen next. He sent the disciples out again with the twelve baskets to pick up the scraps from the ground. People were so full they had left the food where it dropped. Twenty minutes later they were back again with twelve baskets full of bread and fish.

'Remember this,' said Jesus. 'Let's eat.'

He caught sight of me then, lingering when the crowd had gone. 'Is there something you want?' he asked. 'Is it the bread? Are you still hungry?'

'Not exactly,' I said. 'It's a different kind of hunger really. I had it and now it's gone. While I'm with you it's gone.'

And that was the start of it really. I followed him and I knew I was home. The restlessness went. I knew what my life was for and how to live it. There was food and drink every day for the spirit as well as for the body.

Retold from Mark 6.30–44

'I am the bread of life. Whoever comes to me will never be hungry, and whoever believes in me will never be thirsty.'
John 6.35

Sharing together

Pass around some fresh bread warmed in the oven. Share the bread together as you explore the next part of the session.

As a whole group

What strikes you about this story when told in this way? How does it resonate with your own experience of life?

In twos and threes

Talk in twos and threes, each trying to give an example of:

● a way in which God's love has guided you when you were lost

● a way in which God's love has fed and sustained you within.

Part 3 Exploring God's mercy through the death and resurrection of Jesus

A reflection on the passion

As Christians we believe that the place where God's love is revealed and demonstrated is in the passion and death of Jesus our LORD.

To explore God's mercy and the depth of his love for us we need to explore the passion of Christ. It is because of Jesus' death on the cross that we find our direction in life (which is also the way of the cross). It is because of Jesus' death on the cross that all of our hungers can be satisfied in him.

Read the story of the last supper and the institution of Holy Communion in 1 Corinthians 11.23–26:

> For I received from the LORD what I also handed on to you, that the LORD Jesus on the night when he was betrayed took a loaf of bread, and when he had given thanks, he broke it and said, 'This is my body that is for you. Do this in remembrance of me.' In the same way he took the cup also, after supper, saying: 'This cup is the new covenant in my blood. Do this, as often as you drink it,

in remembrance of me.' For as often as you eat this bread and drink the cup, you proclaim the LORD's death until he comes.

The feeding with the Manna in the wilderness and the feeding of the five thousand both help us to understand the gift of Holy Communion.

Jesus gives us this special meal to remember his death on the cross. The bread is a sign of his broken body. The wine is a sign of his blood poured out for us.

These are the signs of God's mercy and love for us. Through them we remember all that Jesus has done.

In the service of Holy Communion we re-centre our lives again on following Jesus and find direction. We receive spiritual food and drink that satisfies. We look forward to the great banquet in heaven.

For discussion

● How do you approach receiving Holy Communion?
  Is this act a living sign of God's love for you?

● What helps as you prepare for the service?

● What new insight about God's mercy are you taking away from this session?

Prayers together

Some wandered in wilderness and desert
They lost their way home to a place where they could live

They were hungry and thirsty
and their life force ebbed away

Then they cried out to the LORD in their distress
He saved them from all their troubles

He led them by a straight pathway
To a place where they could make their home

Let them give thanks to the LORD for he is good
For the wonders he does for the human race

For he satisfies the thirsty soul
And the hungry heart he fills with good things.

Psalm 107.4–9

A time of open prayer or one person may lead prepared intercessions.

Pray for one another and for any questions that have arisen.

Pray for those who are spiritually hungry and spiritually lost.

End with the Lord's Prayer introduced by:

Trusting in the compassion of God,
As our Saviour taught us so we pray:
Our Father in heaven ...

Now LORD you let your servant go in peace;
Your word has been fulfilled.

My own eyes have seen the salvation
Which you have prepared in the sight of every people.

A light to reveal you to the nations
And the glory of your people Israel.

Glory to the Father and to the Son
And to the Holy Spirit
As it was in the beginning, is now
And shall be for ever. Amen

The Song of Simeon

Give thanks to the LORD for he is good
For his mercy lasts for ever

Let the redeemed of the LORD give testimony
Those he has saved from the hand of their enemy

The LORD has gathered us from all the earth
From east and west, from the north and from the chaos of the seas

Let everyone who is wise think about these things
And explore in full the mercy of the LORD

Psalm 107.1–3; 43

For reflection by group members after the session

- Explore God's mercy by reading again Psalm 107.4–9.

- Where are you spiritually hungry or thirsty or restless at the present time?

- Can you turn those longings into prayer?

- What have you learned about God's mercy?

IN PRISON AND SET FREE

notes for leaders

Approximate timings for the session are:

Welcome; opening prayers and reflection	15 mins
Sharing your story	15 mins
Film or song clip	5 mins
A testimony (reading and reflection)	10 mins
Sharing together	20 mins
A reflection on the passion and discussion	15 mins
Final worship and prayers together	10 mins

There is a lot of material in each session so you will need to select from week to week.

Not every group will have 90 minutes available. You could take a couple of evenings over each session. The first would look at the psalm material; the second at the gospel story and the reflection on the passion.

Additional activities

There is a short film clip available on YouTube, and a sound file on the Church House Publishing website, which introduce the session. If you decide to use them, they can be played after the initial reading of Psalm 107. To find the clip on YouTube go to **www.chpublishing.co.uk/exploringgodsmercy** and follow the link. Please visit the same page to find a downloadable sound file you may wish to use instead.

The session suggests making paper link chains with words written on them describing something that holds people captive today. You might want to prepare some of these in advance to add to the effect. You will need enough gummed strips (or cut strips of paper with glue) for each person.

Involving the group

You may want to involve different members of the group in:

● Leading the opening and closing worship.

● Making the paper chains in advance or leading this activity.

● Reading the story (perhaps with several voices).

Other media

There is an excellent and very faithful depiction of Jacob Marley's ghost in *The Muppet Christmas Carol*.

You may be able to think of other clips that illustrate being in prison.

IN PRISON AND SET FREE

Begin with the opening prayers on page 9.

The Song of Freedom

Some sat in darkness and the shadow of death
Held captive by misery and irons

For they rebelled against the words of God
And the commands of the Most High they abandoned

They were bowed down with weariness in their hearts
They fell and there was no one to help them

They cried out to the LORD in their distress
He saved them from all their troubles

He rescued them from darkness and death's shadow
And their bonds he broke apart

Let them give thanks to the LORD for he is good
For the wonders he does for the human race

For he breaks in pieces the doors of bronze
And shatters the bars of iron.

Psalm 107.10–16

Part 1 Exploring God's mercy through the Song of Freedom

I find visiting prisons a sombre experience. On my last two visits I've fallen into what seem at one level like normal, everyday conversations with prisoners only to realize part way through that only one of us is able to go home afterwards and resume normal life. For the other person, most of each day will be spent locked in a small cell with very little freedom allowed and very few visitors.

Most of us, thank God, never experience what it's like to be locked up and in prison. But most of us will find out what it means to be trapped in different ways by our circumstances and unable to escape them. It's very common to feel trapped by debt and by our financial circumstances. Many have been tempted to borrow beyond their means by banks who should have known better. Others fall victim to loan sharks who prey on the most vulnerable.

I've talked over the years to people who feel trapped in their jobs. Something they once enjoyed now seems a drudge. They have been passed over for promotion and life is going nowhere.

Others can feel very trapped at times in relationships that have seen better times or by the responsibilities of family life. Others feel trapped because negative emotions such as depression or anxiety make them a prisoner locked in their own home or into certain patterns of behaviour. There are many ways today of being a prisoner.

This Song of Freedom recognizes all these different ways of being trapped and held prisoner. We saw that the first part of the psalm, the Song of the Pilgrim Way, is deeply rooted in the story of Israel's Exodus from Egypt. Exodus means 'journey out'. On the long journey through the desert the people who were set free depended upon God's grace for guidance in the wilderness and for the gift of food each day.

The Song of Freedom echoes this great Exodus story. The journey from Egypt was also a journey to freedom in the promised land. However, the Song of Freedom also echoes the other profound and transforming experience rooted deep in the minds of the community that first used Psalm 107: the experience of the Exile.

In 587 BC the city of Jerusalem and its temple were destroyed by the king of Babylon. Many of its leading citizens were taken away into exile, not knowing if they would ever see their home again. You can read about the Exile in the historical books of the Old Testament (see 2 Kings 25) and in the prophets (most of the Books of Jeremiah and Ezekiel are set at the beginning of the Exile, and the prophet of Isaiah 40—55 prophecies about the return from captivity). Psalm 137 is one of the songs composed when the people of Jerusalem were held prisoner against their will:

> By the rivers of Babylon, there we sat down and there we wept
> when we remembered Zion.
> On the willows there we hung up our harps.
> For there our captors asked us for songs,
> and our tormentors asked for mirth, saying,
> 'Sing us one of the songs of Zion!'
>
> *Psalm 137.1–3*

After 70 years of exile and against all expectation, the people of Jerusalem were set free and began to return to Jerusalem and to rebuild the city and, eventually, the temple. Anyone singing this part of Psalm 107 in that rebuilt temple would see in the Song of Freedom a reference to exile and to the LORD's deliverance.

However, the Song has a wider reference also. There is literal captivity here but also a more spiritual captivity:

> Some sat in darkness and the shadow of death
> Held captive by misery and irons.
>
> *Psalm 107.10*

Some are literally held captive and the irons that hold them cause misery and plunge them into darkness and the shadow of death. But others find themselves trapped in the circumstances of this life and the fear of death; they are held captive by misery and their experience of living feels exactly like being a prisoner.

It's worth pausing for just a moment on the phrase 'the shadow of death'. This isn't translated very literally in the main English versions. NRSV has simply 'gloom'. NIV has 'deepest gloom'. You have to go back to the old Authorized Version for 'shadow of death'. If you know Psalm 23 at all in the older translations you may recognize the phrase:

> Yea though I walk through the valley of the shadow of death, I will
> fear no evil; for thou are with me ...
>
> *Psalm 23.4, AV*

Being a prisoner is connected here very strongly with being held captive in this life by death, which brings misery and frustration to every human life. It is often the sense that our lives must come to an end, which grows into a sense of being trapped and imprisoned in this life for a time and which makes us feel like prisoners here.

There is a difference between the prisoners and those who are lost. The lost bear no responsibility for their plight: they simply find themselves in trackless wastes. The prisoners, however, are held captive because of their rebellion. Again something of the human condition is caught here.

In some ways we are born into this world and share in the general plight of humanity: its lostness. In other ways we are drawn into suffering and the sense of imprisonment through the chains we make for ourselves through our choices and through our wrong actions.

Charles Dickens' wonderful novel, *A Christmas Carol,* captures this element of chains and judgement brilliantly in the description of Scrooge's former business partner, Jacob Marley, who appears to Scrooge covered from head to foot in shackles:

> The chain [Marley] drew was clasped about his middle. It was long and wound about him like a tail; and it was made (for Scrooge observed it closely) of cash-boxes, keys, padlocks, ledgers, deeds and heavy purses wrought in steel.

Later Marley explains the meaning of his chains:

> 'I wear the chain I forged in life', replied the Ghost. 'I made it link by link and yard by yard; I girded it of my own free will and of my own free will I wore it. Is its pattern strange to you?'

Some chains are hung upon us by others and some we forge ourselves through our own choices. The net result is the same though: a great weariness of heart and spirit and a sense that there is no one who can help us (Psalm 107.12).

But this is not the song of the captives, it is the song of the free. It is the testimony of those who found they were trapped in that place and cried to the LORD in their trouble. They found that their prayers were answered; that God was able to come and set them free from all the chains that were wrapped around them. They were liberated from every oppressor.

Charles Wesley's great hymn, 'And Can It Be', picks up the image, drawing on this psalm and on the two great accounts of Peter and Paul being set free in Acts 12.6–17 and 16.16–34:

Long my imprisoned spirit lay
Fast bound in sin and nature's night;
Thine eye diffused a quickening ray –
I woke, the dungeon flamed in light;
My chains fell off, my heart was free,
I rose, went forth, and followed thee.

Wesley captures in this beautiful image of being set free something deep in the heart of becoming a Christian. To find Christ is to be set free from our chains; free to fly.

John Bunyan's great allegory of the Christian journey, *The Pilgrim's Progress*, uses the image not of chains but of a heavy and backbreaking burden that holds the human spirit down. We are set free in and through the work of Christ on the cross.

Sharing your story

Take some moments once again to reflect on how your life was (or is) without God. You may be able to look back to a time when you were not a Christian. You may not be sure that you are a Christian now.

Tell part of your story to one another using the language of being trapped and in prison. What was it like? How has God set you free?

Can you see anything in your own life similar to Jacob Marley's chains or John Bunyan's great burden?

Do you experience in your Christian life now times when you feel trapped and like a prisoner? How do you deal with this?

You may want to share as a whole group; or one person might prepare in advance and tell part of their story; or you might want to share in twos or threes.

If you are reading this book on your own take some time at this point to journal and look back on the way this sense of being trapped and set free has surfaced in your life.

A film or song clip

See page 28 for suggestions.

Part 2 Exploring God's mercy in the ministry of Jesus

A testimony

One of the group should read the story aloud.

Let me tell you about my brother. It's the saddest and gladdest story I can tell, you see. Sit down. It will only take a few minutes but make yourself comfortable.

We were close when we were growing up. There was just me and him in the family and mum. Dad died when we were small. We did all the normal stuff. Good boys mostly. The odd prank now and again. Nothing too serious.

I'm two years younger than he is. When he was about 15 we started to grow apart. He would go off on his own. At first it was just for an hour or two but then it stretched to half a day then eventually days at a time. He never told anyone what he was doing – not at the time at any rate.

He became more and more distant. We never shared a laugh or anything. I missed him. He'd no interest in the house or the neighbours. Mum worried about him. That was when she turned grey, those years. Then he started to develop this mad look in his eyes. He got more and more withdrawn and solitary. We'd see him less and less.

He stopped washing. His hair and beard grew long. He took to sleeping outside in the summer. He never ate much so he was thin as a beanpole. He lived mostly out among the tombs. Mum reckoned he started going to visit Dad's grave and then it kind of got hold of him really. He couldn't let go, she said.

As if worrying about him wasn't enough, the next summer we started getting complaints. The neighbours would be round. Stuff had been pinched. First eggs or bread. Then it was a chicken or a goat. No one ever knew for sure it was him. But once they started blaming him for one thing he got the blame for the lot. If anything went wrong at all on our part of the shore, it was my brother who got the blame.

Everyone said he was mad or that he had demons. Legion they called him because there were so many of them. He was happiest in the graveyard so we used to tie him up among the tombs. Ropes were no good. He undid them in minutes. So they would forge chains and come and shackle him up.

I got a job looking after pigs near where he was. Mum wanted me to keep an eye on him. I hated the work. No one else would do it. There was a good market in bacon at the Roman garrison.

I'd sit by the shore watching the pigs root about and listening to his cries. He'd gash himself with the rocks trying to get the chains off. He was the strongest man I'd ever seen. He still knew me, just. He'd never hurt me. But no one else could go near him. Mum would bring food up for us both every day. We would leave his near the tombs. It broke our hearts. We wore ourselves out with cries and prayers. Everyone else had given up.

Then one day a boat came ashore – a ferry on its way to Decapolis. Normally they landed further away but these were strangers or perhaps the wind blew them to the shore. A man got out first, the teacher they were all talking about. Word had reached us.

My brother saw the man at once and ran towards him on the shore. I ran after him. I was terrified someone would get hurt. He knew who Jesus was straight away: 'What have you to do with me, Jesus Son of the Most High God? Don't torment me.'

Jesus was speaking to him – or to whatever was holding him prisoner. I was running as fast as I could but I couldn't hear everything Jesus said.

The next thing I knew there was a great cry as if my brother was being torn into pieces. That very same moment there was a great commotion in the herd of pigs. They were about 50 yards away down the shore. The lot of them went completely mad. You never heard such a noise. They ran this way and that screaming, and then, all at once, the whole lot of them ran down over the cliff and into the sea.

The rest of the swineherds were scared stiff, I can tell you. They ran off into the city. I went and got a spare set of clothes I always kept for my brother in case he needed them. By the time the crowds came back, there was my brother, no longer called Legion and no longer a prisoner. He was clothed and in his right mind and sitting at Jesus' feet. We embraced for the first time in four years. It was a miracle.

There was no end of a commotion. What had happened was a good thing but all the people were afraid. They begged Jesus to go away

to the other side again and not come to their city. He did just as
they asked. My brother begged to go with him. He was still afraid
and ran to get into the boat. Jesus took him to one side and looked
at him and loved him and told him to go and tell his story all around
the city. One day Jesus would come back again.

So we went together, from place to place, telling the story of how
we'd both been set free. And everyone – every single person –
was amazed.

Retold from Mark 5.1–20

'I am the resurrection and the life. Those who believe in
me, even though they die, will live, and everyone who
lives and believes in me will never die.'

John 11.25

Sharing together

Pass around some gummed paper for making chains. Work in small groups to
make long paper chains. Write on each piece of paper something that traps and
enslaves people today. Try to make a chain for each member of the group,
which should be worn until the final prayers.

As a whole group

What strikes you about this story when told in this way? How does it resonate
with your own experience of life?

Note the deliberate connection with the Song of Freedom. Compare Psalm
107.10 with Mark 5.4.

In twos and threes

Talk in twos and threes and each try to give an example of

● a way in which God's love has set you free.

Part 3 Exploring God's mercy through the death and resurrection of Jesus

A reflection on the passion

One of the most moving and dramatic scenes in the New Testament is the moment in John's gospel where Jesus calls Lazarus from the tomb. The fourth gospel tells the story very clearly in the language of freedom from chains that bind us, echoing the language of the shadow of death in Psalm 107:

> So they took away the stone. And Jesus looked upwards and said, 'Father, I thank you for having heard me. I knew that you always hear me, but I have said this for the sake of the crowd standing here, so that they may believe that you sent me.' When he had said this, he cried with a loud voice, 'Lazarus, come out!' The dead man came out, his hands and feet bound with strips of cloth, and his face wrapped in a cloth. Jesus said to them, 'Unbind him, and let him go.'
>
> *John 11.41–44*

Jesus' death on the cross sets us free from slavery and imprisonment of every kind. Jesus' death on the cross secures for us the gift of eternal life and sets us free from the imprisonment of death. Jesus' own resurrection is the sign that we shall rise again with Christ and share in the gift of eternal life.

The whole of our lives can be overshadowed by death. Christ's own death has set us free now to live in the perspective of eternity.

Baptism is a sign that we have died with Christ to our old life and that we live already the risen life with him.

For discussion

● What difference does it make to your life now that Christians have been set free from the fear of death and from death itself?

● How will you use your freedom?

● What new insights about God's mercy are you taking away from this session?

Prayers together

The group members have been wearing the chains made in Part 2 during the final part of the session. After you have read the psalm together rip off each other's chains as a sign of the freedom you have in Christ.

Some sat in darkness and the shadow of death
Held captive by misery and irons

For they rebelled against the words of God
And the commands of the Most High they abandoned

They were bowed down with weariness in their hearts
They fell and there was no one to help them

They cried out to the LORD in their distress
He saved them from all their troubles

He rescued them from darkness and death's shadow
And their bonds he broke apart

Let them give thanks to the LORD for he is good
For the wonders he does for the human race

For he breaks in pieces the doors of bronze
And shatters the bars of iron.

Psalm 107.10–16

A time of open prayer or one person may lead prepared intercessions.

Pray for one another and for any questions that have arisen.

Pray for those who are prisoners and held captive physically or spiritually.

End with the Lord's Prayer introduced by:

Trusting in the compassion of God,
As our Saviour taught us so we pray:
Our Father in heaven ...

Now LORD you let your servant go in peace;
Your word has been fulfilled.

My own eyes have seen the salvation
Which you have prepared in the sight of every people.

A light to reveal you to the nations
And the glory of your people Israel.

Glory to the Father and to the Son
And to the Holy Spirit
As it was in the beginning, is now
And shall be for ever. Amen

The Song of Simeon

Give thanks to the LORD for he is good
For his mercy lasts for ever

Let the redeemed of the LORD give testimony
Those he has saved from the hand of their enemy

The LORD has gathered us from all the earth
From east and west, from the north and from the chaos of
the seas

Let everyone who is wise think about these things
And explore in full the mercy of the LORD

Psalm 107.1–3; 43

For reflection by group members after the session

● Explore God's mercy by reading again Psalm 107.10–16.

● Where are you trapped or imprisoned at the present time?

● Can you turn those longings into prayer?

● What have you learned about God's mercy?

SICK AND MADE WELL

notes for leaders

This session explores God's mercy through the picture of being sick and made well.

Welcome; opening prayers and reflection	15 mins
Sharing your story	15 mins
Film or song clip	5 mins
A testimony (reading and reflection)	10 mins
Sharing together	20 mins
A reflection on the passion and discussion	15 mins
Final worship and prayers together	10 mins

There is a lot of material in each session so you will need to select from week to week.

Not every group will have 90 minutes available. You could take a couple of evenings over each session. The first would look at the psalm material; the second at the gospel story and the reflection on the passion.

Additional activities

There is a short film clip available on YouTube, and a sound file on the Church House Publishing website, which introduce the session. If you decide to use them, they can be played after the initial reading of Psalm 107. To find the clip on YouTube go to **www.chpublishing.co.uk/exploringgodsmercy** and follow the link. Please visit the same page to find a downloadable sound file you may wish to use instead.

The gospel story this week is for two voices and people may need notice to read it well.

For the activity, you will need some large pebbles and crayons or felt-tip pens to decorate them. The session notes also suggest having a simple cross to place in the centre of the room during the final prayers.

It may also be appropriate to offer prayer for healing at the end of the session with laying on of hands and/or anointing with oil. You will need to think through in advance how you might do this.

Involving the group

You may want to involve different members of the group in:

- Leading the opening and closing worship.

- Providing the pebbles and pens.

- Providing refreshments.

- Reading the story (perhaps with several voices).

Other media

The singer-songwriter Don Fransisco has a song called 'Gotta Tell Somebody', which is a beautiful and dramatic retelling of the healing of Jairus' daughter.

SICK AND MADE WELL

Begin with the opening prayers on page 9.

> ### *The Song of Wholeness*
>
> Some were sick from sinful ways
> **They were afflicted because of their wrongdoing**
>
> Their soul hated every kind of food
> **They came close even to the gates of death**
>
> Then they cried out to the LORD in their distress
> **He saved them from all their troubles**
>
> He sent out his Word and healed them
> **And saved them from their destruction**
>
> Let them give thanks to the LORD for his steadfast love
> **For the wonders he does for the human race**
>
> Let them offer sacrifices of thanksgiving
> **And tell of all his deeds with joy**
>
> *Psalm 107.17–22*

Part 1 Exploring God's mercy through the Song of Wholeness

Psalm 107 gives us a third picture of God's mercy and love: healing for those who are diseased.

Everyone knows what it's like to be ill. Even if we are spared serious illness, we know what it's like to be laid low with a heavy cold or stomach bug. Our strength is drained away. Our spirits often sink with our physical health. Our appetite for the good things in life as well as food and drink ebbs away. Most of us are miserable company yet need the friendship of others in these times.

Many people of course experience very serious illness in their own lives or else in the lives of those they love. 'Coming close to the gates of death' is all too common, even for those living in a time of excellent medical care and a country where it is readily available and free at the point of need.

In the face of cancer or a sudden serious infection we feel powerless, our defences are stripped away and we feel alone.

The psalm suggests here a very direct link between physical illness and personal sin, which causes that illness. The Bible wrestles in different places and in different ways with this connection. In some places the Old Testament makes the link very explicit (as here). In other places in the psalms, there are loud protestations of innocence. There is a debate going on.

This wrestling in the Old Testament reaches its climax in the Book of Job. Job is a righteous man who suffers acutely in a way he does not deserve. Job's friends repeatedly tell him that he is suffering because of his own sin. Job himself protests his innocence: it is not possible or helpful to read back from a person's sickness or suffering to their own guilt or sin.

The argument rages fiercely through thirty-eight chapters of the book. Job's 'friends' point out with a fierce and compassionless logic that as he is suffering he must have sinned. Job for his part argues back with even greater passion that he is innocent; that he does not deserve this immense suffering.

In the final chapters of the book, the problem of suffering is not finally resolved. The book's answer to the problem is that it cannot be resolved in this life. However, Job is granted a deeper vision of God's nature and activity and majesty which leads him to a new place in trusting in God despite his suffering. His honesty and integrity are vindicated: his suffering is not caused by his own sinfulness. In the final chapter, God says to Eliphaz, the leader of Job's comforters:

'My wrath is kindled against you and against your two friends; for you have not spoken of me what is right, as my servant Job has.'

Job 42.7

According to Job, sickness is not caused directly by sin. We should take very great care therefore not to lay on anyone who is suffering (including ourselves) the additional heavy burden that this suffering is due to their sin.

The same debate continues in the New Testament. There are one or two passages that suggest a direct connection between a person's action and their illness. But the majority view in the New Testament stands with the Book of Job. Jesus makes it absolutely clear in John 9 that the man he heals was not born blind because of either his sin or the sin of his parents (John 9.3):

As he walked along, he saw a man blind from birth. His disciples asked him, 'Rabbi, who sinned, this man or his parents, that he was born blind?' Jesus answered, 'Neither this man nor his parents sinned; he was born blind so that God's works might be revealed in him.'

John 9.1–3

Modern medicine still holds to the view that some illness is clearly caused by poor choices or lifestyle decisions. We can make ourselves ill through overindulgence. We can increase the likelihood of lung and heart disease through smoking. If we keep physically fit we are more likely to be healthy for longer.

The Christian view is, however, that there is normally no moral connection between a person's own sin and any illness they may contract. When we are well, this all sounds very basic and obvious. But sometimes we all may need help understanding this. It remains a very natural human reaction to be angry with God if we or someone we love contracts an illness ('What did we do to deserve this? God must be punishing me').

We need to move on to the view that sickness is not sent by God as a punishment for individual sin. Innocent people suffer. Sickness is part of the groaning of creation; the imperfect state of the world. The world is much less than it could be because of sin. We all share the responsibility for that sin and imperfection. We all contribute to the stock of sin in the world through our own selfishness. God sent his Son to save the world from every imperfection, including sickness and illness. But there is no line to be drawn directly from a person's own sin to their disease.

Jesus healed the sick as a physical sign of God's love restoring all that is lost in an imperfect world. For that reason Christians from earliest times have prayed for the sick. The ministry of healing has been part of the life of the Church in every generation. The prayer and care for the sick has also resulted down the centuries in Christian involvement in the healing professions and in medicine and medical research. Sometimes our prayers for healing are answered directly in ways we cannot understand. Sometimes they may not be answered and physical healing is not given.

This too leaves questions for faith and difficult emotions. We need the love and care of others in those times more than we need neat answers to our questions. We need also to express our pain and grief and questions in prayer to God.

For the core dis-ease of the human soul, however, there is always healing in God's grace. When our souls are sick and diseased because of our sin and the choices we have made, there is always healing and forgiveness in the cross of Christ. Our relationship with God can be forged again because of his love and his grace and his salvation. That healing comes through the Word sent by God.

As a bishop, one of my roles is to license and institute vicars to parishes as they begin a new ministry there. The most solemn part of the service is where I read the licence aloud to the new vicar and then hand it to them with the words: 'Receive the cure of souls which is both yours and mine.'

The phrase 'cure of souls' is an ancient one. It means much more than 'care of souls', which might be expressed through love, listening and affection. It is about the gradual healing and restoration to wholeness that is at the heart of the Christian journey. This cure of souls is at the heart of ordained ministry and all Christian leadership. A local church should be a place where people are growing in spiritual health – where souls are being cured. The cure of souls does not only refer to the time when we come to faith. The cure of souls is a lifelong process. Throughout our whole lives Christ is calling us to deeper and deeper spiritual health and maturity. That journey is a journey from disease to wholeness.

> He sent out his Word and healed them
> And saved them from their destruction
>
> *Psalm 107.20*

As I read this part of the psalm as a Christian, I remember that Jesus is called by St John the Word of God. He is sent by God for the healing of the world; for the ultimate healing of every disease and illness; and to restore and mend my soul and yours.

Sharing your story

Again, look back over the story of your Christian life.

How has your journey of faith been like a journey from spiritual sickness to spiritual health? What kind of medicine has God used?

How have you experienced the cure of souls?

If you can, share some examples of ways in which you have been healed from diseases of the soul. In what ways can you see you have become less proud or selfish or more open to others or more able to forgive?

What means has God used in this journey of healing? Was it the particular words of a friend or counsellor? Was it a moment of grace in the Eucharist or a passage of Scripture? Was it a specific prayer for inner healing?

Where do you need God's grace of healing at this moment in your life and spiritual journey?

You may want to share as a whole group; or one person might prepare in advance and tell part of their story; or you might want to share in twos and threes.

If you are reading this book on your own take some time at this point to journal and look back on the way this sense of being diseased and journeying to wholeness has been part of your own story.

A film or song clip

See page 42 for a suggestion.

Part 2 Exploring God's mercy in the ministry of Jesus

Two of the group should read the story aloud (ideally a man and a woman).

We meet every year on the anniversary of the day he came. Every year we tell the story again. We were both desperate but in different ways.

You were desperate because of the child. Having a daughter so close to death is a terrible thing. The light of your lives. It really looked as though she might die. A child can fall ill so quickly. Laughing one minute. At death's door the next.

And you were so desperate because you'd been ill for so long. Haemorrhages for twelve long years. You'd been ill for as long as our daughter had been alive. Every day of her life, you'd been in pain. Not just in pain either. Cut off from everyone because your illness made you unclean.

It was a terrible time. The loneliness was worse than the bleeding. It twisted me inside. I'd spent everything on the doctors. Nothing left at all. I thought Jesus was my last chance, if ever he came back to our town.

She'd been ill for three days. Each day she grew weaker, slipping away from us. Word reached us mid morning that Jesus had landed on the shore. There was a massive crowd. I couldn't bear to leave her side but my wife made me go. She said Jesus was our only chance.

It wasn't the first time Jesus had been to town. I'd tried to get near him before but I couldn't make it through the crowd. I tried calling out but I was too scared. The last thing I wanted to do was to draw attention to myself.

I'm not ashamed to say I pulled rank. I was one of the synagogue leaders then. I'm not now, of course. They threw me out years ago. But then I was well respected. The crowd made way and let me through. Word had gone round that she was so ill.

I saw you coming through the crowd. I was just trying to get close. You made it look so easy asking Jesus for something. I couldn't have done it.

I couldn't help myself. I'd have done anything. I was a proud man in those days. Full of my own position. But I would have walked over hot coals to get Jesus to come back to my house. I fell at his feet and begged him. I had to ask him four or five times.

Then I saw from where I was standing. He picked you up and set you on your feet and began to come with you. I thought that was my chance. You were leading him in my direction. Even then I was too afraid to speak to him. I thought if I can just touch the edge of his cloak as he passes by. Everyone was jostling him and shaking his hand. He still had lots of friends in this town.

I was trying to lead Jesus through the crowd as fast as I could. He sensed the urgency and was just behind me. Then he stopped.

*I managed to touch that cloak. As soon as I did, the bleeding stopped.
I knew I was better. There was such a sense of peace and joy and hope
again. I think I must have smiled and lifted my eyes up to heaven. And then
I noticed that Jesus had stopped moving and turned round.*

I couldn't believe it at the time. Nothing was more important than getting
Jesus back to my daughter. I pressed him to come on.

*'Who touched my clothes?' he said quietly, looking at the crowd. Of course,
he knew it was me. I shrank back into the crowd. His disciples mocked him:
'Everyone is pressing in on you. How can you say who touched me?'
He kept on looking round.*

I was tearing my hair out by this time – what was left of it. 'My daughter,'
I started to say. Then you moved.

*I couldn't stay quiet. I just had to tell him. I pushed forward again. I was
shaking all over. Just like you I fell on my face before him and told him
everything. I'll never forget his words. In all my life they were the best words
I ever heard. He lifted me up, took my hands in his hands and looked me
straight in the eyes: 'Daughter, your faith has made you well; go in peace
and be healed of your disease.' I stopped shaking. But then the messengers
came.*

My worst fears were realized. They came shouting from the house with
the last words any father ever wants to hear: 'Your daughter is dead.'
They were expecting her to die. 'Why trouble the teacher any more?'

*I was still standing next to Jesus. It all happened so quickly. He smiled at
me, let go of my hands and turned to you: 'Don't be afraid,' he said.
'Only believe.' Then he really seemed to move quickly. He left the rest of the
crowd behind. He just took three of the disciples and went off with you.
I followed behind with the crowd.*

When we got to the house there was already a great commotion. The
professional mourners had arrived. Everything was being made ready for
the funeral. There was wailing in every room. He asked them why and said
she was sleeping. They laughed at him so he put them all outside.

*We arrived just as they were all being turned out into the street. There was
some ripe language being used I can tell you. The crowd sensed something
was going to happen. You could feel it in the air.*

He took me and my wife upstairs with the disciples to where our daughter lay. He took her by the hand and said very simply: 'Little girl, get up.' It was just as though she were waking up after a long sleep. She was back with us. He told us to give her something to eat.

He also told you not to tell anyone. I never really understood that part. The whole town knew she was sick and had died because of the mourners. But it did mean he couldn't come back into the town again for a long time.

We've been friends ever since that day. Every year we tell the story. Every year we remember the healings. Every year we offer thanks for all it means.

Retold from Mark 5.21–43

'Come to me, all you that are weary and are carrying heavy burdens, and I will give you rest. Take my yoke upon you, and learn from me; for I am gentle and humble in heart, and you will find rest for your souls. For my yoke is easy, and my burden is light.'

Matthew 11.28–30

Sharing together

Have some large pebbles and crayons or felt-tip pens available. As you talk together about the stories of healing, everyone should choose a pebble and write on it the things they are carrying in their souls that are a burden and for which they seek healing.

It could be the weight of a persistent illness or the memory of a painful episode. It could be a fault you keep trying to overcome or a weakness or something that needs renewing. The way you decorate your pebble need not be explicit – you could simply use initials or a picture.

As a whole group

Which is your favourite story of Jesus healing someone?

What strikes you about this double story when told in this way? How does it resonate with your own experience of asking Jesus for healing?

In twos and threes

Talk in twos and threes and each try to give an example of

- a way in which God's love has healed your diseases.

Part 3 Exploring God's mercy through the death and resurrection of Jesus

A reflection on the passion

More than five hundred years before Jesus' death, the remarkable prophet who left us the fifteen chapters of Isaiah 40—55 wrote movingly of the death of God's servant who was to come. This prophet describes himself only as a voice. He was writing from the end of the Exile with a prophecy of hope and is sometimes called 'Isaiah of the Exile'.

The death of God's servant is for the benefit of others. Those benefits are described in the language of healing:

> Surely he has borne our infirmities and carried our diseases;
> yet we accounted him stricken, struck down by God, and afflicted.
> But he was wounded for our transgressions, crushed for our iniquities;
> upon him was the punishment that made us whole,
> and by his bruises we are healed.
> All we like sheep have gone astray;
> we have all turned to our own way,
> And the LORD has laid on him the iniquity of us all.
>
> *Isaiah 53.4–6*

There is a profound truth here, which is beyond our analysis and understanding. We are able to understand it only in part and only in pictures. All that Jesus suffered on the cross in some deep and unfathomable way is part of God's purposes that achieves our own healing. Reconciliation between God and humanity is made possible in the sacrifice of Christ.

The physical healings described in the gospels are a sign of this deeper healing accomplished on the cross. The physical healings are made available to some; this deeper healing is made available to all. The physical healings are made available through God's power at work in Jesus' life; this deeper healing is made possible only through Jesus' sacrificial death. The physical healings were limited in time and place; this deeper healing is available at any time and place and lasts for all eternity.

The New Testament writers reflect on and echo this passage in a number of places, most clearly in 1 Peter 2.24:

> He himself bore our sins in his body on the cross, so that, free from sins, we might live for righteousness; by his wounds you have been healed. For you were going astray like sheep, but now you have returned to the shepherd and guardian of your souls.

For discussion

- What difference does it make to your Christian journey that Christ died for your healing?

- What are the next steps in your journey to wholeness and wellbeing in Christ?

- What new insights about God's mercy are you taking away from this session?

Prayers together

The members of the group have been decorating their pebbles during the final part of the session. Set a simple wooden cross in the centre of the room for your prayers. After you have read the psalm together, place your own pebble at the foot of the cross as a sign of seeking God's deeper healing and wholeness.

Some were sick from sinful ways
They were afflicted because of their wrongdoing

Their soul hated every kind of food
They came close even to the gates of death

Then they cried out to the LORD in their distress
He saved them from all their troubles

He sent out his Word and healed them
And saved them from their destruction

Let them give thanks to the LORD for his steadfast love
For the wonders he does for the human race

Let them offer sacrifices of thanksgiving
And tell of all his deeds with joy

Psalm 107.17–22

A time of open prayer or one person may lead prepared intercessions.

Pray for one another and for any questions that have arisen.

Pray for those who are spiritually diseased and need healing.

It may be appropriate to pray for physical healing with laying on of hands or anointing with oil.

End with the Lord's Prayer introduced by:

> Trusting in the compassion of God,
> As our Saviour taught us so we pray:
> **Our Father in heaven ...**

> Now LORD you let your servant go in peace;
> **Your word has been fulfilled.**

> My own eyes have seen the salvation
> **Which you have prepared in the sight of every people.**

> A light to reveal you to the nations
> **And the glory of your people Israel.**

> Glory to the Father and to the Son
> And to the Holy Spirit
> **As it was in the beginning, is now**
> **And shall be for ever. Amen**

The Song of Simeon

> Give thanks to the LORD for he is good
> **For his mercy lasts for ever**

> Let the redeemed of the LORD give testimony
> **Those he has saved from the hand of their enemy**

> The LORD has gathered us from all the earth
> **From east and west, from the north and from the chaos of the seas**

> Let everyone who is wise think about these things
> **And explore in full the mercy of the LORD**

Psalm 107.1–3; 43

For reflection by group members after the session

- Explore God's mercy by reading again Psalm 107.17–22.

- Where do you need to be made well at the present time?

- Can you turn those longings into prayer?

- What have you learned about God's mercy?

STORM TOSSED AND COMFORTED

notes for leaders

This session explores God's mercy through the picture of being storm tossed and comforted.

Approximate timings for the session are:

Welcome; opening prayers and reflection	15 mins
Sharing your story	15 mins
Film or song clip	5 mins
A testimony (reading and reflection)	10 mins
Sharing together	20 mins
A reflection on the passion and discussion	15 mins
Final worship and prayers together	10 mins

There is a lot of material in each session so you will need to select from week to week.

Not every group will have 90 minutes available. You could take a couple of evenings over each session. The first would look at the Psalm material; the second at the gospel story and the reflection on the passion.

Additional activities

There is a short film clip available on YouTube, and a sound file on the Church House Publishing website, which introduce the session. If you decide to use them, they can be played after the initial reading of Psalm 107. To find the clip on YouTube go to **www.chpublishing.co.uk/exploringgodsmercy** and follow the link. Please visit the same page to find a downloadable sound file you may wish to use instead.

The gospel story this week is for two voices or more and people may need notice to read it well.

For the activity, you will need to prepare a piece of paper with a boat in the centre for each small group of two or three. You will also need scissors and paste and a collection of newspapers and magazines.

It may also be appropriate to offer prayer for inner peace at the end of the session with laying on of hands and/or anointing with oil. You will need to think through in advance how you might do this.

Involving the group

You may want to involve different members of the group in:

● Leading the opening and closing worship.

● Providing the equipment for the collage.

● Providing refreshments (fish and chips would give a seaside feel to the session!).

● Reading the story (perhaps with several voices).

Other media

The recent disaster movie *2012* has some very striking scenes of chaos and storm as the earth's crust moves, causing tsunamis and earthquakes.

STORM TOSSED AND COMFORTED

Begin with the opening prayers on page 9.

The Song of Calm

Some went down to the sea in ships
They did their business on the great waters

They saw all the creation of the LORD
They saw his wondrous works in the deep

He spoke and raised up a mighty wind
He lifted up the waves of the sea

They went up to the heavens and down to the earth
Their spirits melted away in their distress

They staggered and fell like drunkards
All their wisdom forsook them

Then they cried out to the LORD in their distress
He saved them from all their troubles

He made a calm upon the storm
And quieted the waves of the sea

Then they rejoiced because they were at rest
And he brought them to the safe harbour they longed for

Let them give thanks to the LORD for his steadfast love
For the wonders he does for the human race

Let them offer sacrifices of thanksgiving
And tell of all his deeds with joy

Psalm 107.23–34

Part 1 Exploring God's mercy through the Song of Calm

The fourth song in Psalm 107 is also the longest. 'The Song of Calm' is the best-known part of the text in Britain. We are an island race with a history of seafaring. The opening lines have been grafted into the minds of previous generations in the older translations: 'Those who go down to the sea in ships and ply their business on the great waters.'

The Victorian hymn 'Eternal Father, strong to save' by William Whiting is still widely used with its memorable chorus: 'And hear us when we cry to thee for those in peril on the sea.' Parts of the second verse of the hymn draw directly on the graphic descriptions of storm and tempest in the Song of Calm.

The original choir who sang this song would be singing to an audience who knew what it was to venture on the seas. The Old Testament contains at least one story of a sea voyage, storm and man overboard in the tale of Jonah and the whale. It would only be a small number of the temple congregation who had ever actually been to sea. However, the psalm would speak about the nature of salvation through this image to everyone who gathered for the great festival.

To understand exactly how, we need to ask what the sea represented in the ancient world. The sea is very familiar in twenty-first century Britain. We enjoy trips to the seaside and gazing across the waters. Travel by ship is relatively safe. We live in an age where the oceans have all been mapped. Navigation is good. The weather is normally known a little in advance. We have even begun to explore the mysteries that lie beneath the surface of the ocean.

None of these things were true in the ancient world. The sea was dark, unknown and unfamiliar. No one knew what lay in the depths of the oceans. The weather was unpredictable. A storm at sea was a terrible prospect. The sea itself seemed boundless for those who ventured beyond the shores of the Mediterranean. For all the people of the Ancient Near East, the sea represented the forces of chaos in a range of different ways.

Think back to the story of creation in seven days in Genesis 1. At the beginning of creation, all is chaos. The earth is without form and void. All is darkness and water covers the face of the deep. When the poets reached for an image to describe what was there before creation, for nothingness, they used the image of a limitless expanse of water. In the seven days of creation, God brings order out of this chaos.

On the first day, God speaks and light comes into the darkness. Light and darkness are separated into night and day. On the second day, God speaks and from the waters creates the sky and the ocean. On the third day, God speaks and separates the ocean from the dry land and sets the boundaries for the sea. These verses were never intended to give a literal or scientific account of seven days of twenty-four hours in which God made the world. They describe much deeper truths that lie at the foundation of creation. Creation brings order from the forces of chaos.

The creation stories developed by other nations in the Ancient Near East describe long battles between the gods of order and the forces of chaos, which are represented by great sea monsters. The Old Testament writers are inspired to see that the sea is a part of God's good creation: it is not a god. Nevertheless it remains the part of creation that is most dangerous and unpredictable. It most symbolizes chaos, danger and disorder. The great sea monster in Job 40 has been of created by the LORD. There is no part of creation that is beyond the LORD's goodness or influence. But the chaos monster remains something to be feared by God's people.

Genesis also tells the story of God's destruction of humanity. The means of destruction is a great flood. Noah is saved from the chaos and destruction of the great waters by means of the ark. The ark story remains a powerful one and has recently been retold in two feature films: *Evan Almighty* and the disaster movie *2012*.

In the prophecies of Isaiah of the Exile, the Israelites are assured of God's great love and that his love and strength will remain with them even when they pass through deep waters – a symbol borrowed from the journey through the Red Sea and which gains its power from this idea of the water as chaotic and dangerous:

> But now thus says the LORD, he who created you, O Jacob,
> he who formed you O Israel:
> Do not fear, for I have redeemed you; I have called you by name,
> you are mine.
> When you pass through the waters, I will be with you;
> and through the rivers, they shall not overwhelm you …
>
> *Isaiah 43.1–2*

So the people who first sang this song may not have known what it was like to be in a storm at sea. However, every one of them would have known what it was like to be subject to forces of chaos in this world beyond their control: to be taken up to the heights and brought down to the depths. They would know what it feels like when your spirit or your courage melts away before these powerful forces of disorder beyond your own control. They would know that feeling when wisdom or skill disappears and you are left naked before the storm, at the end of your own resources.

They would have prayed to the LORD in those moments and many would have experienced salvation and God's mercy as peace and calm in the midst of life events that feel like storms. Many would have experienced the deep inner peace that comes from God's presence in difficult situations. Many would have known the stilling of the outer storms as order emerges from chaotic lives.

In many ways human life today is very different. We seem to have much more control over our environment. But the images of chaos and storms remain very helpful in making sense of life. Many people do experience chaos and storm in all kinds of ways. Natural disasters strike in different parts of the world and we see through our television screens or through relatives and friends caught up in those disasters the chaos that they bring to carefully ordered human communities. In our own country we are subject to greater and greater extreme weather events. Last year I was taken to visit someone in Sheffield who had been affected by the massive floods in the city a few years ago. I was shown the place six feet up on the living room wall in an ordinary home where the flood water reached in just a few hours. I was told of the chaos and devastation that followed.

It's not difficult, then, to imagine that kind of physical chaos invading our lives. It happens to people we know. It is much more common, of course, to experience at some point inner chaos and being subject to forces beyond our control. In the present recession, many people have had their homes repossessed or their life savings affected by events in the global economy. The decisions that led to these events were taken in boardrooms in Manhattan or Kuala Lumpur, way beyond their own control. Still others lose their jobs and their futures because of decisions taken by multinational companies on the other side of the world they can do nothing about. The forces of chaos break in.

Many people's lives are affected by mental illness or conditions of various kinds, which disable them either in very public ways or more personal ones. It feels to people in those circumstances that the forces of chaos are just under the surface, waiting to break through. Others are drawn into addictions to habits such as gambling or the regular abuse of alcohol or drugs, which, as it were, unleash the forces of chaos within their emotional lives and work and families. Still other people are subject to multiple pressures of poverty and peer pressure and difficult family backgrounds. They often describe their lives as chaotic. As soon as one thing is put right or help is received in one area, the chaos and disorder pulls them down in a different direction. Still others experience chaos in their lives or health or inner calm through bereavement or serious illness; through redundancy or through relationship breakdown.

As we have seen in earlier parts of Psalm 107, there are many ways to describe salvation. We can describe it as the lost being found and the hungry fed. We can describe it as those in prison being set free. We can describe salvation in the language of the diseased being made whole. The Song of Calm tells us that we can see salvation in this powerful fourth picture of those overwhelmed by chaos and disorder finding peace, security and safe harbour.

How does this happen? In two ways. A life lived without reference to God can be a life that is in chaos, blown this way and that by every desire and temptation. Paul writes in Ephesians of the need for Christian maturity and he uses the language of the boat driven by the wind:

> We must no longer be children, tossed to and fro and blown about by every wind of doctrine, by people's trickery, by their craftiness in deceitful scheming.
>
> *Ephesians 4.14*

The Christian faith revealed in Holy Scripture and supremely in the life, death and resurrection of Jesus does bring order to lives that otherwise would be in chaos and peace to those who would be in inner turmoil. Our faith gives us a balanced, true and ordered way of seeing the universe as a whole. We see the creation not as a random accident but something with inherent beauty, order and morality. Our faith gives us also a balanced, true and ordered way of seeing our own place within that universe. We are not insignificant specks of matter floating in an immense darkness. We are created by a loving God for God's good purposes. We were meant to be here and each of us has a calling, a role to fulfil.

When Paul deliberately uses the language of a new creation in the New Testament he is drawing attention to exactly this aspect of salvation:

> So if anyone is in Christ, there is a new creation: everything old has passed away; see, everything has become new!
>
> *2 Corinthians 5.17*

Our understanding of what Christian faith means is enriched by this image of the storm. The peace we know in Christ is like the calm we experience after a storm when wind and waves are stilled. It is the peace where our spirits and our courage return. It is a place where wisdom and equilibrium are restored. It is a place from which we can move forward again. It is a place that we can describe as a safe harbour.

Everyone who becomes a Christian shares in this great movement from chaos to order; from being storm tossed to being centred and having inner peace. Sometimes that movement takes many years. The storm and chaos do not subside instantly.

However, in every Christian life there are also many smaller movements. Order and peace may be great gifts from God but they are also qualities into which we grow and which can from time to time be disrupted by the outward events or inner turmoil in our lives.

Jesus uses the imagery of the storm to describe this kind of movement. At the end of the Sermon on the Mount he tells the story of the two housebuilders. One builds on rock, the other on sand. The lesson is that trouble and chaos come in every life (even the lives of his followers). However, the more deeply we know and put into practice Jesus' own words, the deeper the foundation of our lives and the better we are able to stand against the storm's effects:

> 'Everyone then who hears these words of mine and acts on them will be like a wise man who built his house on rock. The rain fell, the floods came, and the winds blew and beat on that house, but it did not fall, because it had been founded on rock.'
>
> *Matthew 7.24–5*

The more we practise Christian disciplines, the more we will be anchored in the storm. The same point is made by what seems to many a long and otherwise curious passage in the Acts of the Apostles. Chapter 27 in Acts is largely taken up with an extended and detailed account of a storm at sea, which culminates in Paul landing on the island of Malta. Luke is normally quite economical in his language. What is the point of telling us about this very long storm at sea?

One of its lessons, almost certainly, is God's ability to bring salvation and deliverance to disciples and to the Church as a whole through the most severe storms – both literal and metaphorical. Many times on this journey, Paul's ship seems about to run aground or be broken up by the wind and waves. However, Paul himself is brought through the crisis. In the same way, however hard-pressed we are, however much the forces of chaos press in, however overwhelmed we seem to be, hope remains as a firm anchor for the faith that we will come through the storm to safe harbour (Acts 27.1–44). In the words of the letter to the Hebrews:

We have this hope, a sure and steadfast anchor of the soul ...

Hebrews 6.19

Sharing your story

As you look back over the story of your Christian life can you see how you have been travelling from being storm tossed and blown about to a place of peace and inner calm?

Is it possible to identify both a larger movement and more recent episodes where you have felt this?

What are the elements in life you are most conscious of that build chaos in people's lives? What are the elements that most bring order?

You may want to share as a whole group; or one person might prepare in advance and tell part of their story; or you might want to share in twos and threes.

If you are reading this book on your own take some time at this point to journal and look back on the way this sense of being diseased and journeying to wholeness has been part of your own story.

A film or song clip

See page 56 for a suggestion.

Part 2 Exploring God's mercy in the ministry of Jesus

One or more of the group should read the story aloud. Change voices with each new line.

> We were always crossing Galilee. Every other day at one point or another.

> *Jesus had to keep moving by that stage to stay ahead of the crowds.*

> And it was a lot quicker than walking after a long day. His teaching sessions would last for hours. Not that people wanted to go home.

So what was he talking about that day?

All those parables of the kingdom I think. He would tell the stories to the crowd and then unpack them a bit when we were all in the boat. Remember?

I remember you could never get what they meant. We had to explain the sower to you seven times.

I'm not the only one. Anyway, we were there all day and it was getting dark. Jesus wanted to go across the lake.

I think sometimes he just needed to get away from the crowd.

We all got into the boats.

That didn't stop other people following us though. There were about a dozen or so boats I think.

We set off across the lake. Then all of a sudden this wind came up out of nowhere.

It often does on Galilee. You get no warning at all.

The waves were getting higher. Most of us were used to the lake but this was really bad. The lamps went out and it was pitch black. Sheets of rain.

We were soaked in no time.

We tried everything.

The waves came higher and higher over the top of the boat.

We were spun around. We could hear the people in the other boat but we couldn't see them.

I thought we'd all had it that night. You would be up one minute down the next.

Except for Jesus.

Slept through it all from beginning to end. He was worn out.

But we woke him in the end. It was either that or a watery grave. We were being driven before the wind.

We were a bit sharp when we woke him. Anyone would have been: Teacher don't you care we are perishing?

It wasn't just us though. All those other boats would have gone down as well. I never would have set off in that weather.

Anyway Jesus stood up in the boat. He held on to the mast. He sort of rebuked the wind and shouted at the sea.

Peace. Be still.

It stopped. Just like that. In an instant.

Dead calm on the outside.

Deep peace on the inside.

Jesus sat down. We just looked at him.

Why are you afraid? Have you still no faith?

He'd seen our faces. I don't think he minded us being afraid of the storm.

He was telling us not to be afraid of him. He must have seen it in our faces. He could still the waves.

It was just like the psalm: he made a calm upon the storm and quieted the waves of the sea.

But we knew that only God could do that. Only God could bring us to safe harbour.

Retold from Mark 4.35–41

'Be still, and know that I am God!'

Psalm 46.10

Sharing together

Divide the group into twos and threes for this exercise. Give everyone a sheet of A4 paper on which you have drawn a small boat in the centre (about 3 cm across). If you can't draw a boat then find a picture in a magazine and stick it on.

You will need lots of old newspapers and magazines, some scissors and some glue. Ask each group of two or three to make a collage around the boat of headlines, pictures and stories that contribute to storms and chaos in peoples lives.

As you make the collage talk together about your response to the story. What would it have been like to be there? What lessons do you think Jesus wants the disciples to learn?

Share a little, if you can, of the storms you have known in your own life and any experiences of coming into calm and safe harbour.

Part 3 Exploring God's mercy through the death and resurrection of Jesus

A reflection on the passion

Paul writes a great deal in his letters about peace. This peace is one of the fruits of the Holy Spirit in Galatians 5. It is an inner, personal quality; a state of inner harmony and wellbeing found in Christ. However, peace is also a community quality; something we are to strive for in our churches and in our relationships in wider society. It is the inner calm that individuals and communities need to enjoy life and to function well.

In this passage in Ephesians, Paul writes very movingly about the way in which this peace flows directly from the death of Jesus on the cross. It is one of the many benefits of his passion. Because Christ died on the cross there can be a double reconciliation; a double stilling of the storm.

We can be reconciled to God and so find the deep, inner calm of knowing our creator and our purpose and destiny. We can also be reconciled to others in families, communities and races.

This could not have happened apart from the death of Jesus, God's son, on the cross. Paul writes:

But now in Christ Jesus you who once were far off have been brought near by the blood of Christ. For he is our peace; in his flesh he has made both groups [Jews and Gentiles] into one and has broken down the dividing wall, that is, the hostility between us.

He has abolished the law with its commandments and ordinances, so that he might create in himself one new humanity in place of the two, thus making peace, and might reconcile both groups to God in one body through the cross, thus putting to death that hostility through it.

So he came and proclaimed peace to you who were far off and peace to those who were near; for through him both of us have access in one Spirit to the Father.

Ephesians 2.13–18

For discussion

● What difference does it make to your Christian journey that Christ died to bring calm to the storm; order from chaos and peace where there is division?

● What are the next steps in your journey towards calm, order and peace in your own life and in your church community?

● What new insights about God's mercy are you taking away from this session?

Prayers together

Before you pray, have a few minutes of quiet and move around the room looking at the different collages you have made.

Some went down to the sea in ships
They did their business on the great waters

They saw all the creation of the LORD
They saw his wondrous works in the deep

He spoke and raised up a mighty wind
He lifted up the waves of the sea

They went up to the heavens and down to the earth
Their spirits melted away in their distress

They staggered and fell like drunkards
All their wisdom forsook them

Then they cried out to the LORD in their distress
He saved them from all their troubles

He made a calm upon the storm
And quieted the waves of the sea

Then they rejoiced because they were at rest
And he brought them to the safe harbour they longed for

Let them give thanks to the LORD for his steadfast love
For the wonders he does for the human race

Let them offer sacrifices of thanksgiving
And tell of all his deeds with joy

Psalm 107.23–34

A time of open prayer or one person may lead prepared intercessions.

Pray for one another and for any questions that have arisen.

Pray for those who are storm tossed and need God's comfort.

It may be appropriate to pray for inner peace with laying on of hands or anointing with oil.

End with the Lord's Prayer introduced by:

Trusting in the compassion of God,
As our Saviour taught us so we pray:
Our Father in heaven ...

Now Lord you let your servant go in peace;
Your word has been fulfilled.

My own eyes have seen the salvation
Which you have prepared in the sight of every people.

A light to reveal you to the nations
And the glory of your people Israel.

Glory to the Father and to the Son
And to the Holy Spirit
As it was in the beginning, is now
And shall be for ever. Amen

The Song of Simeon

Give thanks to the Lord for he is good
For his mercy lasts for ever

Let the redeemed of the Lord give testimony
Those he has saved from the hand of their enemy

The Lord has gathered us from all the earth
**From east and west, from the north and from the chaos of
the seas**

Let everyone who is wise think about these things
And explore in full the mercy of the Lord

Psalm 107.1–3; 43

For reflection by group members after the session

● Explore God's mercy by reading again Psalm 107.23–34.

● Where do you need calm, order and peace at the present time?

● Can you turn those longings into prayer?

● What have you learned about God's mercy?

SESSION **5**

LIVING THE FRUITFUL LIFE

notes for leaders

This final session explores God's mercy through the picture of living a fruitful life. Approximate timings for the session are:

Welcome; opening prayers and reflection	15 mins
Sharing your story	15 mins
Film or song clip	5 mins
A testimony (reading and reflection)	10 mins
Sharing together	20 mins
A reflection on the passion and discussion	15 mins
Final worship and prayers together	10 mins

There is a lot of material in each session so you will need to select from week to week.

Not every group will have 90 minutes available. You could take a couple of evenings over each session. The first would look at the psalm material; the second at the gospel story and the reflection on the passion.

Additional activities

There is a short film clip available on YouTube, and a sound file on the Church House Publishing website, which introduce the session. If you decide to use them, they can be played after the initial reading of Psalm 107. To find the clip on YouTube go to **www.chpublishing.co.uk/exploringgodsmercy** and follow the link. Please visit the same page to find a downloadable sound file you may wish to use instead.

The gospel story this week is for two voices and people may need notice to read it well.

For the activity you will need a range of different kinds of fresh fruit in season to make a fruit salad for the group to share. You may well have your own recipe but an easy way to make a fruit salad is to open a large can of pineapple cubes in juice; tip them into a bowl and then add the different chopped fruits.

Members of the group will need sharp knives; peelers; chopping boards and so on. You will also need to provide a way for the group to wash their hands before and after chopping.

The idea is to make the fruit salad part-way through the session and then eat it together after the final prayers so you will need bowls and spoons for that. Whether or not you serve it with cream is up to you!

Involving the group

You may want to involve different members of the group in:

- Leading the opening and closing worship.
- Providing the fruit and equipment for making the salad.
- Providing refreshments.
- Reading the story (perhaps with several voices).

Other media

As a way of summing up the whole series, use Neil Diamond's song, 'Pretty Amazing Grace'.

LIVING THE FRUITFUL LIFE

Begin with the opening prayers on page 9.

The Song of Fruitfulness

He turns rivers into deserts
And springs of water to thirsty ground

A fruitful land becomes a salty waste
Because of the wickedness of those who live there

He turns the desert into pools of water
And thirsty ground becomes springs of water

The hungry come to live there
They establish a city to inhabit

They sow fields and plant vineyards
They bear fruit in abundance

He blesses them and they multiply abundantly
And their cattle do not decrease

When they are diminished and brought low
Through oppression, trouble and sorrow

He pours contempt on princes
And they wander in trackless wastes

But he raises up the poor from their distress
And makes their families like flocks

The righteous see this and rejoice
And all wickedness shuts its mouth.

Psalm 107.33–42

Part 1 Exploring God's mercy through the Song of Fruitfulness

We have explored God's mercy through the pictures of being lost and found; hungry and well fed. We've looked at the images of being in prison and set free; being sick and made well; getting caught in a storm and finding safe harbour.

The final song in Psalm 107 is different from the others. We have heard the four songs of testimony of those who gathered 'from east and west, from the north and from the chaos of the sea' (v. 3). Each of these songs has the same refrain, as we have seen:

> Then they cried out to the LORD in their distress
> He saved them from all their troubles.
>
> *Psalm 107.6*

and then a few verses later:

> Let them give thanks to the LORD for he is good
> For the wonders he does for the human race.
>
> *Psalm 107.15*

The final song has a very different form. All the others are really short stories – narratives about particular groups of people. We identify in different ways with their journey from a bad place (lost; in prison; sick; storm tossed) to a good place (home; freedom; health and safe harbour). We see these great images and journeys reflected in the gospel accounts of Jesus. Jesus the good shepherd finds the lost. Jesus sets the captives free. Jesus heals the sick. Jesus calms the chaos of the storm.

The songs give us physical pictures of inward and spiritual realities. These pictures all become part of the way the early Christians talk about salvation.

And so, in turn, these great images become windows to help us to reflect on God's mercy and the wonders he has done for us. They are ways of seeing and describing our own salvation.

But the final section of the psalm is not a story or a testimony in the same way. It doesn't describe the plight and rescue of any particular group. Instead the song is a series of statements about God. Even though the LORD is not named here, he is the person who acts, the subject of each of the verbs.

However, the imagery in this final part of the psalm remains strong (and different from each of the other four songs). At first this final section can seem like a random collection of images and pictures. But there is, I think, a unifying theme that gives us a fifth great image of God's mercy and of salvation. It is the image of the barren becoming fruitful: the image of the good and abundant life.

As with the other songs, there is a sense in which the bad state is described before the good state. The first two sections of the song talk about God turning rivers into deserts, springs of water into thirsty ground and fruitful land into a salty waste.

Ancient Israel was of course an agricultural society in a climate where nothing would grow unless there was water, either from rainfall or from irrigation. The difference rain or the lack of rain made to what grew was profound. The consequence of no rainfall was significant and immediate hardship.

These early first verses of the psalm echo an ancient story. Genesis tells us about the destruction in Abraham's time of the cities of the plain and the creation of the barren Dead Sea and the salty wastelands that surround it. Everyone in Jerusalem would know the tale and the landscape which is only a day's journey from the city. They would remember as well the stories in the Old Testament of drought caused by God because of wickedness in the land – and especially the stories of Elijah told in I Kings 18. Elijah's great, defining battle is with the prophets of Ba'al, the Canaanite God of fertility and rain.

In the psalms, this picture of dry ground has become a powerful metaphor for our relationship with the living God:

> O God, you are my God, I seek you, my soul thirsts for you;
> my flesh faints for you, as in a dry and weary land where there is no
> water.
>
> *Psalm 63.1*

Most of us realize when we read these words the deep longing for God implied by dryness and thirst. We may not realize the longing for fruitfulness that God's presence makes possible. This is a cry from a barren heart and life to be watered so that good things can grow.

After these initial couplets, Psalm 107 then completely reverses the imagery. Not only does God turn springs of water into thirsty ground, he also does the opposite:

> He turns the desert into pools of water
> And thirsty ground becomes springs of water.
>
> *Psalm 107.35*

This in turn leads to a virtuous circle of fruitfulness and prosperity. Water attracts people who are hungry. The hungry build a city; sow fields; plant vineyards. The fruitful life is established around the oasis God has provided.

> They bear fruit in abundance
> He blesses them and they multiply abundantly.
>
> *Psalm 107.38*

Again there are rich biblical echoes here. Throughout the Exodus stories, the promise held before the Israelites on their journey through the wilderness is that God will bring them to a fruitful land, a land flowing with milk and honey. God demonstrates his power over nature from the beginning to the end of this journey with spectacular miracles in which water bursts from the rocks or is discovered in desert places.

The vision of the good life in the Hebrew Scriptures is expressed from beginning to end in terms of fruitfulness, from Adam and Eve in the fruitful garden in Genesis 2 (and the command to be fruitful and multiply) to the vision of perfection where 'shall sit every man under his vine and under his fig tree' (Micah 4.4, AV). The profound picture of the river of life flowing from the temple in Ezekiel 47 is a picture of God's grace transforming a barren landscape (and barren lives) to fruitfulness once again. A trickle of water flowing from the temple represents God's grace flowing into both lives and societies that are rightly ordered. That trickle becomes first a stream then a great river. Wherever the river flows there is abundant and fruitful life.

God is the one who has the power to reverse what is happening in nature – to make the barren fruitful – and to reverse what is happening in human society. The existing order can be overthrown:

> He pours contempt on princes
> And they wander in trackless wastes
> But he raises up the poor from their distress
> And makes their families like flocks.
>
> *Psalm 107.40–41*

Compare Luke's echo of these words in the Song of Mary:

> He has brought down the powerful from their thrones,
> and lifted up the lowly;
> he has filled the hungry with good things,
> and sent the rich away empty.
>
> *Luke 1.52–53*

This picture of the fruitful life is of course widely taken up in the teachings of Jesus and the rest of the New Testament. Jesus himself tells, as we shall see, parables about seed growing and land becoming abundantly fruitful. He presides over a miraculous harvest from the sea.

In John's gospel, Jesus echoes Psalm 107 and Ezekiel 47 when he speaks of streams of living water flowing from within the heart of the believer:

> 'Let anyone who is thirsty come to me, and let the one who believes in me drink. As the scripture has said, "Out of the believer's heart shall flow rivers of living water."'

John 7.37–38

God's grace working in the barren life of the believer will produce a fruitful life. In John 10, we have Jesus' promise of fruitfulness and purpose:

> 'I came that they may have life, and have it abundantly.'

John 10.10

In John 15, with the wonderful image of the vine, there are again many references to 'bearing fruit'. Fruit in the Bible means a range of different things. It can mean a changed society (as in Isaiah 5). It can mean inner change: the fruits of the Holy Spirit (as in Galatians 5.22ff.); it can mean a great harvest for God's kingdom – the growth of the church (as in Matthew 9.37–38).

Human life, as we have seen, is a search for direction; a search for freedom; a search for health; a search for calm and stability. All of these qualities are part of what Scripture means by salvation. God in his mercy and love promises all of them. We receive these gifts in part in this life and fully in the life to come.

However, human life is also a search for fruitfulness, for abundance. This is sometimes distorted into a desire for an abundance of possessions or status or power or influence. However, there is also a deeply rooted, God-given longing in each person in creation to live a life that bears fruit, which makes a difference, and is given purpose and meaning through the fruit we bear.

This longing to bear fruit and make a difference is seen in the desire to have children and see them grow to maturity. It is seen in people's longing for fulfilment in the work that they do. People long not simply to be employed or to have work that suits their gifts, but to be involved in producing or making something that is worthwhile. We see the same God-given longings in the creative arts; in cooking; in gardening; in design; in music. There is deep satisfaction in creativity and fruitfulness – in making and seeing the product of our labours. To make and produce different things is part of what it means to be human.

This means in turn that many people are dissatisfied with their lives and own an inner restlessness because their lives feel barren. It may be a literal barrenness – the inability to conceive a child – which is one of the hardest challenges life brings. It may be a sense that the work we do is pointless and without meaning, or that the way we spend our time does not satisfy.

To become a Christian is to discover that God in his mercy and grace has not created us to be consumers in society or pew fillers in the church. God has called us to be partners and co-workers. He has meaningful work for us to do according to the gifts and abilities he has blessed us with. To be a Christian is to consecrate our lives to his service and seek to discover at each stage of our lives our proper calling to fruitful work.

The first four songs of Psalm 107 each look back: they are songs of testimony to God's goodness and each helps us to explore his mercy. However, this final song in its way looks forward to the rest of our lives. What kind of soil are we called to be? Barren? Or abundant?

Sharing your story

As you look back over the story of your Christian life can you identify times when that life was barren and times when you have borne fruit? Where do you think you are in this present season?

What do the barren times have in common? What about the fruitful times? Are there lessons you can share with one another?

You may want to share as a whole group; or one person might prepare in advance and tell part of their story; or you might want to share in twos and threes.

If you are reading this book on your own take some time at this point to journal and look back on the way this sense of being diseased and journeying to wholeness has been part of your own story.

A film or song clip

See page 72 for a suggestion.

If you are using the Neil Diamond song, 'Pretty Amazing Grace', it may be better at the end of the session as part of the final prayers.

Part 2 Exploring God's mercy in the ministry of Jesus

The story this week is for a couple of voices reading alternate paragraphs.

One of the things I remember most about travelling with Jesus was that every day brought surprises.

We'd wake up in the morning and think to ourselves: we're going to go to such and such today and it will go like this. More often than not the opposite happened.

Remember that time we went to Nazareth?

Everyone thought it would be the triumphant homecoming – entertained by all the family and friends.

Jesus was looking forward to it. He wanted us all to meet the family.

We had a good couple of days' rest. It all went quite well until the Sabbath.

Jesus got up to speak in the synagogue. Before he was five minutes in there were mutterings and murmurings.

Where did he get all this? Who does he think he is?

He's just a carpenter. We know his brothers and sisters.

Nothing happened really – nothing to compare with what we'd seen in Galilee.

Even Jesus was amazed that day – but at their unbelief not their faith.

He redoubled his teaching after that. He really focused on getting around the villages and talking to people.

That was when we had another surprise. We thought we were there just to listen – to take it all in.

Little did we know. It was around that time he started to send us out two by two.

We normally went ahead of him on the road everywhere where he might go. We would go to a place, find someone to stay with and then talk to them about Jesus and preach the good news.

He gave us a staff for the journey but no money.

We had the gospel.

And we had some oil to anoint anyone who was sick.

And that was another surprise. When we prayed, they started to get better. We started to see people being set free. We saw people's lives changed.

Then when Jesus came in a few days' time, the way was prepared.

And we went on doing it month after month until we'd been round the whole of Galilee. It was amazing. It set the pattern for the rest of our lives.

Retold from Mark 6.1–13

> 'I am the vine, you are the branches. Those who abide in me and I in them bear much fruit, because apart from me you can do nothing.'
>
> *John 15.5*

Sharing together

Make a fruit salad together as a group. Have a selection of seasonal fruit with some water, bowls and sharp knives. Try and involve everyone in peeling the oranges; slicing the melon; peeling and slicing mango or kiwi fruit. Put the prepared fruit into a single large bowl.

You will need to think through where to put the rubbish and also have some way for people to wash their hands both before and after cutting up the fruit.

As you talk together, reflect a little on your response to the story. What's your favourite kind of fruit? What's your favourite kind of spiritual fruit: a changed life; a changed society or a growing church?

Does the Christian life feel to you more like being a spectator in the synagogue at Nazareth or being on the road as a disciple in Galilee? Are you commentating on the performance of others or getting involved yourself?

Share a little about the times you feel you have been most fruitful as a Christian.

What do you think you may need to do to get back on track and bear fruit again? How can this group help?

Once you've made the salad and washed your hands finish this part of the discussion and move onto the next. Serve and eat the fruit together after the prayers.

Part 3   Exploring God's mercy through the death and resurrection of Jesus

A reflection on the passion

Jesus uses many images and pictures to speak about the meaning of his death. One of them is the picture of the grain of wheat in John 12.24:

> 'Very truly, I tell you, unless a grain of wheat falls into the earth and dies, it remains just a single grain; but if it dies, it bears much fruit.'

There is a paradox – something very unexpected – in what happens to a grain of wheat. By sowing it in the earth, the farmer loses it. The grain itself comes to an end. But from the grain comes a root, then a shoot, then a stalk and an ear and finally a rich harvest of many other grains: enough to eat and have enough left for the next season's planting.

Jesus' death on the cross looked like the end of his mission. It looked as though the people of Nazareth were right. Nothing good was going to come of this. There were a tiny number of disciples. Even they were scattered and afraid.

Yet because of Jesus' death the Christian community – the Church – was born. Jesus' presence in the world was multiplied scores of times, then thousands of times, then millions of times in every generation.

In some ways, Jesus' death on the cross is absolutely unique. There was no other death like it.

But in this matter of fruitfulness, Jesus' death is meant to set the pattern. After the verse about a grain of wheat falling into the earth, Jesus goes on:

Those who love their life lose it and those who hate their life in this world will keep it for eternal life. Whoever serves me must follow me, and where I am, there will my servant be also.

The path of fruitfulness is often the costly and sacrificial path for the Christian disciple.

For discussion

● What difference does it make to your Christian journey that God intends your life to bear fruit?

● Have you known seasons of fruitfulness and seasons of resting in the vine?

● What new insights about God's mercy are you taking away from this session?

Prayers together

Before you pray, spend a few moments in quietness and rest and look at the different kinds of fruit you have enjoyed together.

He turns rivers into deserts
And springs of water to thirsty ground

A fruitful land becomes a salty waste
Because of the wickedness of those who live there

He turns the desert into pools of water
And thirsty ground becomes springs of water

The hungry come to live there
They establish a city to inhabit

They sow fields and plant vineyards
They bear fruit in abundance

He blesses them and they multiply abundantly
And their cattle do not decrease

When they are diminished and brought low
Through oppression, trouble and sorrow

He pours contempt on princes
And they wander in trackless wastes

But he raises up the poor from their distress
And makes their families like flocks

The righteous see this and rejoice
And all wickedness shuts its mouth.

Psalm 107.33–42

A time of open prayer or one person may lead prepared intercessions.

Pray for one another and for any questions that have arisen.

Pray for those whose lives are fruitful at present and for those passing through a barren time.

It may be appropriate to pray for particular needs with laying on of hands.

End with the Lord's Prayer introduced by:

Trusting in the compassion of God,
As our Saviour taught us so we pray:
Our Father in heaven ...

Now LORD you let your servant go in peace;
Your word has been fulfilled.

My own eyes have seen the salvation
Which you have prepared in the sight of every people.

A light to reveal you to the nations
And the glory of your people Israel.

Glory to the Father and to the Son
And to the Holy Spirit
**As it was in the beginning, is now
And shall be for ever. Amen**

The Song of Simeon

Give thanks to the LORD for he is good
For his mercy lasts for ever

Let the redeemed of the LORD give testimony
Those he has saved from the hand of their enemy

The LORD has gathered us from all the earth
From east and west, from the north and from the chaos of the seas

Let everyone who is wise think about these things
And explore in full the mercy of the LORD

Psalm 107.1–3; 43

For reflection by group members after the session

● Explore God's mercy by reading again Psalm 107.33–42.

● Where do you need to develop a fruitful and abundant life at the present time?

● Can you turn those longings into prayer?

● What have you learned about God's mercy in this session and this series of sessions?